Success at Cambridge English: Proficiency Writing

Tips and guided practice for the CPE Writing test

Text copyright © 2015 Anna M Rowe

All rights reserved. This book or any portion thereof may not be reproduced or used in any manner whatsoever without the express written permission of the author except for the use of brief quotations in a book review.

Dear Reader

Welcome! I assume you are reading this book because you have decided to take the Cambridge English: Proficiency exam. So let me begin by saying 'Well done!' Cambridge English: Proficiency is the highest English language exam available so your English must be very good already. And you've probably worked hard to get here. However, your work isn't quite done, yet. The Writing test is not easy and most people (even native speakers) would probably find it hard without any preparation. This is where *Success at Cambridge English: Proficiency Writing* comes in. I will guide you through this book and help you prepare for your Cambridge English: Proficiency Writing test. The book is divided into two sections:

Tips: This is where you'll find answers to many questions I've been asked over the years by students. I've also outlined common mistakes students make and how you can avoid them. It's a good idea to read this section before you start on the guided practice questions.

Guided practice questions and sample answers: There are six guided practice questions in this book, covering all question types in the Cambridge English: Proficiency Writing test. It's best to do them in order. When you have completed a guided practice question, compare it to the sample answer. This will help you assess your own work. It's a good idea to edit your original answer at this stage and see how you can improve it.

I hope you enjoy this book and find it useful. Good luck with your exam!

Anna Rowe

Contents

TIPS FOR THE CAMBRIDGE ENGLISH: PROFICIENCY WRITING TEST 6

Format of the Writing test	6
Set texts	6
Word count	7
British English/American English/slang	8
Timing	8
Marking	9
Practicalities	9

GUIDED PRACTICE QUESTIONS AND SAMPLE ANSWERS 11

Part 1: the compulsory essay	11
Sample answer: Part 1 the compulsory essay	16
Part 2: an article	19
Sample answer: Part 2 an article	24
Part 2: a letter	26
Sample answer: Part 2 a letter	31
Part 2: a report	34
Sample answer: Part 2 a report	39
Part 2: a review	42

Sample answer: Part 2 a review 47

Part 2: set text essay 50

Sample answer: Part 2 set text essay 54

Tips for the Cambridge English: Proficiency Writing test

Format of the Writing test

The Writing test is 1.5 hours long and will come after the Reading and Use of English test and before the Listening test. There's usually a break between the tests and you might be able to get a coffee or have a few moments in the fresh air. Ask your exam centre about it. Psychologically, it's always a good idea to know exactly how the day will run.

Within the 1.5 hours you have to answer two questions. You can spend 45 minutes on each question or you might find that you can do one question in 30 minutes and need a whole hour for the other question. This is entirely up to you, but practise, so you don't end up spending too much time on Part 1 and then run out of time in Part 2. Most students find they need roughly the same time for both questions. Both parts are worth the same number of marks.

Part 1 is a compulsory essay question. That means you will definitely have to write an essay. We'll look at essay writing in more detail in the Guided Practice section.

In Part 2 you have a choice of five questions. You need to pick one. The options that may come up are an article, a letter, a report and a review. You may not get all text types. For example, there may be two letters, a report and two reviews. Two questions are based on the Cambridge English: Proficiency set texts. We will look at all text types in the Guided Practice section.

Set texts

The set texts for January 2016 until December 2017 are *Family Album* by Penelope Lively and *The Great Gatsby* by F. Scott Fitzgerald. In Part 2, two questions are based on the set text. You may be asked to write an article, a letter, a report, a review or an essay. For example, you may be given the option of writing an essay on *Family Album* or a letter about *The Great Gatsby*. You can only answer these questions if you've read the books and are very familiar with them. You don't have to read these books in order to do well in the Cambridge English: Proficiency Writing test, but if you haven't read them, there are only three questions left for you to choose from.

Reading one or both of the set texts is great exam preparation. Both books will help you in your Reading and Use of English exam and hopefully help you improve your vocabulary in general. However, it does take time and you will have to read them very carefully in order to understand and answer the questions well. It's your choice whether you read these books or not, but do not try to answer the questions related to them if you haven't.

Word count

The word count is clearly stated on your test, so you don't need to memorise it, but you will need it to practise. You are expected to write 240-280 words in Part 1 (the compulsory essay) and 280-320 words in Part 2. If you are taking the test on a computer there will be a word count on your screen, so you can easily see how much you've written.

If you are writing the test on paper you'll need to know how much space 240-280 words and 280-320 words take up in your handwriting. You won't have time to count words in your exam, so simply count a few of your practice essays and see how many pages you'll have to write. The exam paper is lined A4 paper. Use similar paper for your practice and you'll know exactly what you have to aim for.

Many students get really worried about the word count, but you really shouldn't. You'll need to write a minimum of 240 or 280 words in order to give a full answer. Anything much less than that and you're probably missing a lot of important points. Many students have the opposite problem. They would find it really easy to write many more than 280 or 320 words. But you don't have the time and it's really important that you check your work at the end. So train yourself to be concise. It's good practice, not just for the exam, but also for life.

And let me tell you a secret – the examiners won't count your words. They know how long an answer should be. They mark Writing tests all day, they know very quickly if your answer is too short or way too long. The word count is there to help you stay on track and not lose sight of your timing. So don't worry about it, but use it to help you.

British English/American English/slang

Students can get very worried about whether they should be using British or American English. The truth is, it doesn't matter. Depending on where you've learned English, you may well be using a mixture of both or you may be using a more international English. That's all fine. However, when it comes to spelling you should be consistent within each spelling rule. So, if you spell *organize* in the American way *-ize*, you should also spell *recognize* that way. If you spell *centre* the British way *-re*, you should also spell *theatre* that way. But you can use *organize* (American English) and *theatre* (British English) in the same essay. Just remain consistent within each spelling rule.

Students ask me about slang all the time. They are worried that examiners might not know it. The truth is, the examiners will most likely know the slang, but in the Cambridge English: Proficiency Writing test it's highly unlikely that any slang would be appropriate in any of the tasks. You typically have to write formal letters, articles for journals, essays for your teacher, etc. None of these would warrant the use of slang. I would strongly advise you to avoid slang.

Timing

This is one of the hardest issues for most students. You have a lot to do in 1.5 hours. It will help you to have a clear strategy about how you will spend your time. Here's a suggested outline – feel free to adapt it to make it work for you.

Part 1

Read the instructions, read both texts, underline key language in the texts. (10 minutes)

Think of the key message you want to include in your essay, think of the order in which you want to present your argument. (2-5 minutes)

Write your essay. (25 minutes)

Part 2

Read the questions and choose ONE to answer; consider the text type (article, letter, report, review, essay) AND the topic of the question to make the best choice for you. (5-10 minutes)

Think of the key ideas you want to include in your answer, think about how you will structure your writing. (2-5 minutes)

Write your answer (25-30 minutes)

Read through **both your answers**, checking for errors; edit if necessary. (10-15 minutes)

Do not attempt to write a rough draft and then the full answer. You don't have time. All planning should happen during your preparation before the exam and quickly in your head before you start writing.

Marking

The examiners are looking at four key areas in your written answers. These areas are content, communicative achievement, organisation and language.

Content
The examiners check whether you have done what you were asked to do. For example, have you written a report about a student exhibition as you were asked in the question and did you include all relevant content points.

Communicative Achievement
The examiners think about whether you have written appropriately. For example, if you were asked to write an article for an academic journal your writing should be formal, academic and have an appropriate title.

Organisation
The examiners expect your writing to be logical and ordered in a way that makes sense.

Language
The examiners want to see a high level of grammar and vocabulary used accurately. This includes spelling.

Practicalities

If you're taking the paper-based exam, you have to write your answer in pen (not pencil). You'll have the question paper in front of you, and the answer sheet. The examiners only look at what you've written on the answer sheet, so make sure you write on the answer sheet not the question paper! The answer sheet is lined A4 paper. I recommend that you write on alternate lines, leaving one line blank in between each line you write on. That way, you can easily cross out a word or part of the text and write the corrected version above it. The examiners are used to crossed out sentences and amendments on the text and they are adept at reading different handwriting. However, if your handwriting is illegible, consider taking the computer-based exam.

Guided Practice Questions and Sample Answers

Part 1: the compulsory essay

In Part 1 you are given two short texts on the same topic. You will have to write an essay, summarising and evaluating the key points in the texts and also give your own opinion. Remember, you only have about 45 minutes to do all this. So let's get started.

Look at the guided practice question, particularly the key words in bold. Think about how you would answer it.

> Read the two texts below. Write an **essay summarising** and **evaluating the key points** from **both texts**. Use your **own words** throughout as far as possible, and include your **own ideas** in your answers. Write your answer in **240 – 280 words** on the separate **answer sheet**.
>
> **Arts education matters**
> Recent research suggests that arts in education are closely linked to almost everything that we want for our children: academic attainment, emotional and social development, civic engagement, and equitable opportunity. Exposure to the arts is linked to gains in maths, reading, cognitive ability, critical thinking, and verbal skill. Several studies suggest that arts learning can also improve children's concentration, confidence, motivation and ability to join in teamwork. Despite this, governments are often reluctant in providing funding for arts programmes in schools, thus contributing to the widening gap of attainment between the rich and the poor, as typically children from affluent families are exposed to the arts, whether they are provided in schools or not.
> **Educational division: core vs. additional subjects**
> Educational policy makers like to focus on things easily measured and evaluated, leading to schools focussing on maths, reading and writing. However, are we losing sight of some of the most pleasurable experiences whilst aiming to reach ever higher scores in what is commonly referred to as the 'core' subjects? Whilst reading, writing and maths are, of course, of utmost importance, is it not our duty to allow children to also feel the thrill of performing on stage, enjoy

the feel of paint on their hands and feel connected to their peers when singing in a choir?

Are you ready to write your essay? Before you start, here are a few points for you to think about.

The two texts
Read the two texts carefully and write down the key points. What are the texts about? Do they express similar or different ideas? What are your own ideas about the topic?

Structure
Your essay should have a clear structure:

Introduction
Your introduction should be short – about 20-40 words. It should include what the two texts are about and what your main idea about them is.

Main Body
This should be one or two paragraphs. You must summarise the key points from the texts and evaluate them. When evaluating them include your own opinions and personal views. You don't have to talk about text one and then text two in turns. It's more important that you develop your main idea about the topic and the key points into a clear argument.

Conclusion
Your conclusion should be very short and simply sum up your main argument.

Language
You are asked to write an essay. This means the language you use should be neutral or formal (not informal). **Don't** use idioms (Arts education is ~~a double-edged sword~~), phrasal verbs (This idea has ~~taken off~~) or contractions (Governments ~~can't~~ help the situation). It's also not typical to use the first person singular (*I, me, my*) in essays, so avoid it if you can. In an essay evaluating and summarising two texts, you will probably need to use present tenses (to summarise) and modal verbs, such as *should, may, might, would* and *could* (to evaluate).

Now write your essay. You've already spent time thinking about it. Set yourself a time limit of 45 minutes. When you have finished writing your essay, count your words and see if your essay is too long or short. Set the timer again and spend 15 minutes reading through it and check your spelling and punctuation (capital letters, apostrophes, commas, etc.). Read through your essay carefully and check subject–verb agreement, tenses and word order as well as singular and plural nouns.

Ok, have you finished your essay? Look at the sample answer and compare your writing.

Sample answer: Part 1 the compulsory essay

Here's the question again with the key ideas underlined. Did you focus on similar points?

> Read the two texts below. Write an **essay summarising** and **evaluating the key points** from **both texts**. Use your **own words** throughout as far as possible, and include your **own ideas** in your answers. Write your answer in **240 – 280 words** on the separate **answer sheet**.

> **Arts education matters**
> Recent research suggests that <u>arts in education are closely linked</u> to almost everything that we want for our children: <u>academic attainment, emotional and social development, civic engagement, and equitable opportunity</u>. Exposure to the arts is linked to <u>gains in maths, reading, cognitive ability, critical thinking, and verbal skill</u>. Several studies suggest that arts learning can also <u>improve children's concentration, confidence, motivation and ability to join in teamwork</u>. Despite this, <u>governments are often reluctant in providing funding for arts programmes in schools</u>, thus contributing to the <u>widening gap of attainment between the rich and the poor</u>, as typically children from affluent families are exposed to the arts, whether they are provided in schools or not.
> **Educational division: core vs. additional subjects**
> <u>Educational policy makers like to focus on things easily measured and evaluated</u>, leading to schools focussing on maths, reading and writing. However, are we losing sight of some of the most pleasurable experiences whilst aiming to reach ever higher scores in what is commonly referred to as the 'core' subjects? <u>Whilst reading, writing and maths are, of course, of utmost importance, is it not our duty to allow children to also feel the thrill of performing on stage, enjoy the feel of paint on their hands and feel connected to their peers when singing in a choir?</u>

Read the sample answer and comments below. Is your answer similar or different? In what ways? If you were writing the question again, what would you change? When you have completed this task, put your essay away for a few days. Then try writing it again, this time in 30 minutes.

Essay

Both texts discuss the importance of arts education in schools. This essay aims to summarise the key arguments and evaluate them in the context of arts education in schools today.

> Comment: The topic (*the importance of the arts in education*) is clearly identified in the introduction and the aim of the essay is stated.

Schools are caught in a dilemma about whether to focus on three academic subjects (reading, writing and maths) or whether to make time for arts subjects, such as music, drama and art. Governments and policy makers demand measurable results, which are easier to compile from certain subjects than others. This has led to a strong emphasis on reading, writing and maths, often at the expense of arts subjects. Yet might there not be a way to accommodate both those striving for clear academic measures and comparisons and those placing value on the arts?

> Comment: This paragraph summarises the second text. Notice how key words from the input texts have been reworded (*Governments and policy makers demand measurable results, This has led to a strong emphasis on ...*) The final sentence in the paragraph links the ideas of text 2 to text 1 and creates a logically developed argument.

Studies have highlighted the symbiotic relationship of arts and academics. Exposure to and involvement in arts, such as playing in an orchestra, performing in a play or creating a collage from found objects are not only fun experiences for children, they also benefit from them enormously. Focussing on the arts in school has shown that pupils, amongst other things, have higher academic achievement in the core subjects, concentrate better and become more motivated. It is also one of the ways that the attainment gap between affluent and disadvantaged children can be closed, which is something most governments should take into serious consideration.

> Comment: This paragraph summarises and evaluates the first text and offers the writers own opinion (*something most governments should take into serious consideration*). Notice how key language from the input text has been reworded (*...the symbiotic relationship of arts and academics, ... they*

also benefit from them enormously, ... amongst other things, have higher academic achievement in the core subjects, concentrate better and become more motivated.)

In conclusion, the debate about whether to spend time and resources on core or additional subjects should be redundant. Valuing the arts in schools has far-reaching benefits and thus merits our attention and funding.

Comment: The short conclusion summarises the main idea and offers the writers personal opinion on the topic (... *thus merits our attention and funding*).

Part 2: an article

One of the possible Part 2 questions is writing an article. Here's a sample question. Think about how you would answer this. What are the key words in this question?

> An online travel magazine is compiling a top 10 list of sights in your country. The magazine has asked readers to send in articles on their favourite sight, for example a building or a natural feature. You decide to write an article in which you describe your favourite sight, explain why it is your favourite sight and assess its significance for the people in your country.
>
> Write your article in 280-320 words.

Here are the key words

online travel magazine: This tells you about who is reading your article.

your country: This is meant to make it easy for you. You can choose any sight in your country. But if you know a sight from another country well and want to write about that, that's fine. The examiner won't know where you are from when they are marking.

articles on their favourite sight: This tells you what you need to write.

describe your favourite sight, explain why it is your favourite sight, assess its significance for the people in your country: These are the three content points you will need to cover. Most tasks in Part 2 will have 2-4 content points you will need to include. If you only describe it, but don't mention why you like it, you will not get top marks.

article in 280-320 words: This tells you the text type again and the word count.

Target audience

One of the key aspects students get wrong is that they don't think about who they are writing for. This question asks you to write an article for a travel magazine. Travel magazines are read by the general public. They are not academic and, as the magazine is an online magazine, the reader can quickly choose to click on something else. It's therefore important to capture the reader's attention quickly and keep his/her interest.

Features of an article

Title

An article always needs a title. An article aimed at the general public needs to have a catchy title. Titles aren't easy to write. Often it's best to leave the title until you've written the article then add it. You might be able to use a quote from your own writing. Don't forget to leave a space for it.

Attention grabbing opening paragraph

You can capture your reader's attention in many ways. Here are a few examples:

- describe a scene vividly and clearly
- tell a short anecdote to draw the reader in
- ask a (hypothetical) question

Final thought

Articles don't typically have a conclusion, but they may end on a final thought, for example: *That's why the Colosseum holds such sway over the people of Rome and all of Italy* or *The White Cliffs of Dover will always have a special place in many British hearts.*

Content points

You are given clear content points you must cover in this article. If you miss any out, you will not get top marks. The content points for this question are

- describe your favourite sight
- explain why it's your favourite sight
- assess its significance for the people in your country

You don't have to answer these points in order. You can reorder them however you wish, but you must include them. Don't worry whether you remember exact facts about your favourite sight. The examiners aren't interested in your world knowledge, they want to see how good your English is. So you can just invent details if necessary.

Language

The language you are expected to use depends on the question. In our example, the language shouldn't be formal and needs to include lots of description and personal opinion. However, a different type of article may demand a different type of language. In the exam you are expected to adapt your use of English effortlessly to the topic and question.

Now write your article. You've already spent some time thinking about it. Set your timer for 35 minutes and stop writing then. When you have finished writing your article, read through it and check your spelling and punctuation (capital letters, apostrophes, commas, etc.). Read through your article carefully and check subject–verb agreement, tenses and word order as well as singular and plural nouns. Make sure you have included all three content points and that you are close to the word count.

Ok, have you finished your essay? Look at the sample answer and compare your writing.

Sample answer: Part 2 an article

Here's the question again with the key points underlined.

> An <u>online travel magazine</u> is compiling a top 10 list of sights in <u>your country</u>. The magazine has asked readers to send in <u>articles on their favourite sight</u>, for example a building or a natural feature. You decide to write an article in which you <u>describe your favourite sight, explain why it is your favourite sight</u> and <u>assess its significance for the people in your country</u>.
>
> Write your article in 280-320 words.

Read the sample answer and comments below. Is your answer similar or different? In what ways? If you were writing the question again, what would you change?

When you have finished, put the article away. Try to do the same task again in a few days' time, but allow yourself only 25 minutes to do the writing. Compare your original article to your new article. Can you see any improvement?

Secrets of the stones

> Comment: The article has a slightly mysterious title, which doesn't give too much away.

An expanse of rolling, green hilltops. A wide open bright blue sky. The air is perfectly still. Out of the grassy expanse rise enormous, dark grey stones arranged in a circle. I half expect a prehistoric man to appear in the distance, spear in hand, ready to hunt. But this is 2015 and as I drive on I come to the ticket office with its throngs of people – buses of school children, cyclists braving the hills of Wiltshire, families, history buffs and pensioners on a day out. We've all come to see Stonehenge, one of the most significant prehistoric sites in Britain, if not the whole world.

> Comment: In the opening paragraph the writer describes her favourite sight (in this case the prehistoric site of Stonehenge). But before the writer tells us which famous sight she's chosen, she describes it vividly. By describing the other visitors to the monument, she also begins to answer the final content point (its significance to the people in her country).

Why do I along with my fellow visitors still treasure this old collection of stones? Well, simply because it's not only that – a collection of stones – but so much more. Stonehenge is a ring of giant stones dating back around 5000 years. In its picturesque setting in the English countryside it is an imposing structure – the stones being taller than two people standing on top of each other – and is clearly visible from quite a distance. Whilst the structure is both impressive and scenic, the real significance of this Neolithic site lies in the relationship many Brits have with it. Stonehenge is full of mystery and magic. Who were these people who managed to carry enormous slabs of stone over great distances with no modern technology? Why did they go to the trouble? Theories range from Stonehenge being a giant calendar to it being a site of worship for our forbearers. The lack of definitive answers encourages one to speculate, theorise and discuss the possibilities. Only the stones know their secrets. It makes the place feel special, perhaps spiritual.

> Comment: This paragraph describes the sight in more detail, and gives reasons why the writer loves it. It also explains its significance to the British people. The writer has of course not had time to research the topic. She remembered that it's 5000 years old and when she visited the sight, she saw that the stones were taller than two people standing atop each other. Remember, you want to show the examiner how much English you know, not which facts you can remember, so it doesn't really matter if they are 100% accurate. Perhaps Stonehenge is 4500 years old. It doesn't matter.

So why do we love Stonehenge? Because it connects us to our ancestors. This is where we're from. This, more than cups of tea and cucumber sandwiches, is truly British.

> Comment: The final thought clearly addresses the final content point and rounds off the article nicely.

Part 2: a letter

Another possible Part 2 question is writing a letter. Here's a sample question. Think about how you would answer this question.

> A recent newspaper article discussed the threat of technology taking over our homes and lives. You think that the views expressed in the article were one-sided and have decided to write a letter to the editor. You want to highlight the benefits of technology in our daily lives.
>
> Write your letter in 280-320 words.

Before you start writing your letter, let's think about what's required for this task. Who are you writing to? Which three content points do you have to cover?

Target audience

Who are you writing this letter to? To the editor of a newspaper. However, ultimately letters to the editor are written for publication in the newspaper. You are addressing one person, but really you are addressing all the readers of the newspaper.

Content points

The content points for this task are:

- you are **responding** to a published article
- you think **the article was one-sided**
- you want **to highlight the benefits of technology in our daily lives**.

In this task you must respond to an article. You haven't of course read the article, as it doesn't exist. This means you need to think of what the article may talked about and respond to that. Many Writing tasks require a certain amount of imagination and creativity. You may love letter writing but find this topic very tricky. If this happened in the exam it would be best to choose another question. It's important to consider both the text type (i.e. letter) and the topic (i.e. technology in our daily lives).

Features of a letter

Greeting

A letter to the editor, like any other letter, needs a greeting. Different newspapers have different conventions. *Dear Sir/Madam* is common, *Dear Editor* is also fine. Do not start with ~~To Whom It May Concern~~ or ~~Dear Mr X~~.

In the exam, you may be asked to write a letter to the director of a company or the head of a school. In that case it is best to start with *Dear Mr Smith / Dear Mrs Woods*. You may not be given a name, but think about the situation. If you are likely to know the name were this a real life situation, invent one in the exam.

Reason for writing

Most letters begin by giving a reason for writing. In the case of writing a letter to the editor, you need to make clear reference to the article you are responding to. As in this sample question, you may not be given any details, so you must invent them.

Follow-up

To conclude your letter it is common to ask for some follow-up or action. You may also thank the reader for taking the time to read your letter.

Salutation

As with the greeting, each letter needs a salutation. A safe option, suitable for almost all Cambridge English: Proficiency letters is *Regards* or *Kind regards*, which are both formal, but not overly so. Personal letters can be concluded with *Love,* though it is highly unlikely that you will have to write a personal letter in the exam.

Addresses

Students often waste valuable time making up and writing down addresses. You do not need to include addresses in your exam. You won't lose marks if you do, but you are also not gaining anything. As it wastes valuable time, I strongly suggest you do not write addresses on your letter.

Language

The language you are expected to use depends on the question. However, most letters you are asked to write in the exam will be formal.

As it is a letter, you should use the first person plural (*I, me, my*) and state your personal views. Linking words are useful in letters, but do not overuse them. It makes your writing simplistic.

Now write your letter. Time yourself. How long did you need to write it in full? When you have finished writing your letter, read through it and check your spelling and punctuation (capital letters, apostrophes, commas, etc.). Read through your article carefully and check subject–verb agreement, tenses and word order as well as singular and plural nouns. Make sure you have included all three content points.

Ok, have you finished your essay? Look at the sample letter and compare your writing.

Sample answer: Part 2 a letter

Read the question again and notice the highlighted key words. Did you focus on the same aspects in your letter?

> A recent **newspaper article** discussed **the threat of technology taking over our lives**. You think that **the views** expressed in the article **were one-sided** and have decided to **write a letter to the editor**. You want to **highlight the benefits of technology in our daily lives**.
>
> Write your **letter in 280-320 words.**

Read the sample answer and comments below.

Dear Sir

> Comment: An appropriate greeting. The writer imagined writing to *The Times,* where the editor is a man, hence *Dear Sir*.

It was with great interest that I read your feature on the invasion of technology in our daily lives in last Monday's Lifestyle section. You certainly raised some salient points. I found the example of the fully-automated cup of coffee particularly interesting. Perhaps giving instructions to your coffee machine via your smartphone from bed to have the perfect cup of coffee waiting for you when you get into the kitchen really does take away from the simple pleasure of grinding beans, hearing the water percolate through your machine and the first smell of coffee hitting your nose.

> Comment: The first sentence makes clear reference to the article the writer is responding to. Some details are invented, to make the letter sound natural (*last Monday's Lifestyle section*). The writer refers to specific details in the article (*the cup of coffee*). Of course no one has ever read this article as it doesn't exist, but that doesn't matter. You need to imagine that you have read an article on the threat of technology taking over our lives. In order to respond to the article, you need to invent what it might have been about. Useful phrases

> include *It was with great interest that I read ..., You certainly raised some salient points, I found ... particularly interesting, Perhaps ... does take away from...*

However, I do believe <u>the points of view expressed in the article</u> were rather unbalanced. It is easy to have a nostalgic view of the past (or even the present) when we <u>are faced with</u> such rapid changes in our everyday lives due to the incredible advances in technology. **Yet before** we start <u>waxing lyrically</u> about the traditional way of making coffee, **would it not** be prudent to think of all the benefits technology continues to bring? In my view one of the greatest advantages of new technology is <u>the immediate access to</u> a world library – and **not just** of printed books, **but also** films, music, talks and discussions. You may <u>find this sharing of information invasive,</u> stating that it is no longer possible to have a conversation with the people in the same room as you, as everyone is <u>engrossed in</u> their personal devices. These situations may occur, **but what about** the times when classrooms interact with teachers from across the world? When musicians perform together virtually without boundaries? Or when I simply can find exactly the shop or restaurant I was hoping to find **due to** a few taps on a screen? These are real, everyday benefits experienced by millions of people around the globe. I expect that a newspaper of your calibre would want to include a more balanced view in your feature articles.

> Comment: In the main paragraph the writer states his reasons for disagreeing with the article. Again, he invents concrete points he can disagree with (*conversation with people in the same room*). He also backs up his view points with specific examples (*students/teachers, musicians, finding restaurants*). The final sentence is a suitable follow-up for a letter to the editor. You don't write to the editor to elicit a personal response. You write because you want to raise a point or make a change to the newspaper. There is a lot of rich language in

this letter. Look at the underlined vocabulary and try to incorporate it in your own writing. Read the paragraph again and notice the linking words in **bold**.

Regards

Thomas Beckley

Comment: A suitable salutation concludes the letter.

Is your answer similar or different? In what ways? If you were writing the question again, what would you change?

Now put your letter away for a few days. Then write it again and compare your original letter to your new one. Have you improved?

Part 2: a report

A report is written for a clearly specified audience. Take a look at this question and think about who you are asked to write the report for and why.

> You've recently attended a team building day organised for staff of the company you work for. Your manager has asked you to write a report on the day. You should briefly describe the event and identify the most and least valuable aspects of the day. You should also evaluate the team building day overall and make recommendations on whether it is worth repeating this exercise in the future.
>
> Write your report in 280-320 words.

Before you write your report, let's think about how you can approach this task.

Target audience
You are writing the report for your manager. You may be asked to write a report for a supervisor, a teacher or even a group of people, such a sports society.

Aim of the report
The aim of this report is to decide whether to repeat a team building day in the future. It's important that you have the aim of the report clearly in mind before you start writing.

Features of a report

Title
Every report needs a title. The good news is that report titles are very easy. A good report title is simply *Report into* ___, in this example it would be *Report into staff team building day*.

Introduction
The introduction to a report is very formulaic (meaning you can memorise and use it). A good introduction to a report is *The aim of this report is to evaluate/summarise/propose* ___.

Sub-sections

Reports need clear sub-sections with suitable subheadings. The subheadings are usually very simple. For example in this example they could be *The Event, Highlights, Areas to improve* or *Team Building Day, Positives, Negatives*

Conclusion

The conclusion of a report is often a recommendation or your overall finding of whatever it was you reported on. You should give it a subheading, which can be simply *Conclusion*, but may also be *Recommendation* or *Evaluation*.

Content points

You are given clear content points you must cover in this report. The content points for this question are

- you should briefly describe the event
- you should outline the most and least valuable aspects of the day
- you should give your recommendation on whether to repeat the day or not

You need to invent the details of the event. Be as specific as you like. Reports usually include dates, venues, who was there, etc.

Language

The language of a report is always factual and formal, though not academic. Do not include descriptive or colourful language. Include facts and figures if relevant. Do not use the first person plural (*I, me, my*), instead express your ideas in the passive or in indirect ways (*it is important, that..., there is a need for ...*). Typically a report discusses something that has happened in the past, so use the past tense. For your recommendation, use suitable language such as *(... would be suitable, ...should..., ... would be beneficial)*

Now write your report. Write your subheadings first to help you structure your writing. Set your timer for 30 minutes. When you have finished writing your report, read through it and check your spelling and punctuation (capital letters, apostrophes, commas, etc.). Check subject–verb agreement, tenses and word order as well as singular and plural nouns. Make sure you have included all content points and finished with a clear recommendation.

Ok, have you finished your report? Now read the sample answer and compare your writing.

Sample answer: Part 2 a report

Read the question again. The key points have been highlighted for you. Did you include all of them in your report?

> You've recently attended **a team building day** organised **for staff of the company you work for**. **Your manager** has asked you **to write a report** on the day. You **should briefly describe the event** and **identify the most and least valuable aspects of the day**. You should also **evaluate the team building day overall** and **make recommendations on whether it is worth repeating this exercise in the future**.
>
> Write your **report in 280-320 words**.

Read the sample answer and comments below. Did you use bullet points? If not, rewrite your answer to include bullet points. Do you think this improves your report?

Report into staff team building day

Comment: The report starts with an appropriate title.

This report aims to evaluate the staff team building day run on 25 September for 12 members of the sales team of AdvaTech Divisions.

> Comment: The introduction is one short sentence stating the aim of the report. It includes some factual details (date, number of attendees, name of the company). Do not write things like *for some members of our company*. You would never read that in a real report. Just make up numbers, names, etc.

The Event

The team building day was run by Closer Companies, a consultancy specialising in corporate events and team building exercises. It took place on our premises during normal office hours. The invited members of the sales team were asked to participate in a number of mainly game-based tasks. Refreshments were provided throughout the day.

> Comment: Each section has a suitable subheading. The event is described briefly, addressing the first content point. Again, specific details have been invented (the name of the

consultancy firm). The simple past is used to describe events that happened in the past, and frequently the passive voice is used (*was run, took place on, were asked, were provided*).

Highlights

- Most activities were engaging. It was clear how they would help us work better as a team and how this could lead to better sales.
- The organisers changed the participants around, so everyone got to work with each other at some point during the day. This was a good opportunity for forging closer working relationships with colleagues.
- Staff talked about how excited they were to try out new ideas in the coming weeks. The training day created a buzz in the office.

Comment: The writer chose to write the highlights in bullet form. This is not necessary for all reports, but it works well here. Three positive points are detailed. The second content point is covered here and in the next section. Again, the passive continues to be used when appropriate. Useful vocabulary includes *engaging activities, lead to better sales, change participants around, forging closer working relationships, created a buzz*.

Areas to improve

- It was unfortunate that not all members of the sales team could attend, as this led to a certain amount of division within the team before and after the event.
- The pace of the activities was not always right. Closer Companies did not seem to be aware of how experienced our sales force is, hence spending too much time on fairly basic sales techniques.

Comment: Bullet points are also used for the negative aspects of the event. Notice that instead of saying ~~All members should have attended~~ the writer says *It was unfortunate that ....* A report should not place blame, simply raise concerns. The writer uses *hence* instead of *therefore*, a very high level linking word.

Recommendations

AdvaTech Divisions could benefit from this type of team building day in the future. However, only if the entire sales force were able to attend. By inviting only half the team, this team building day has been more divisive than unifying. In addition to opening up the training day to the whole team, any provider of this service should also be clearly briefed so they are aware of the level of expertise in our organisation.

> Comment: The report finishes with clear recommendations which relate directly to the advantages and disadvantages outlined in the previous sections. The recommendations are not personal, they are an evaluation of the facts. The final content point is covered here. A nice expression used is *more ... than ...*, as in *more divisive than unifying*.

Part 2: a review

One of the options in Part 2 is a review. You may be asked to write a review of a film, book, album, art exhibition or restaurant. Most students find reviews impossible to write unless they really have something to say. A lot of detail is necessary, so it's hard to completely invent a review from nothing. In the exam, read the question carefully and decide if you have enough to say on the given question. For example, if you are asked to write a book review of your favourite children's book, can you remember a children's book clearly enough to write about it? If you cannot, I recommend you choose a different option for Part 2.

Now look at this question. What are you asked to review and who are you writing for? Note down the key words.

> A travel magazine is planning to run a feature on the best restaurants in your area and has asked readers for submissions on their favourite local place to eat. You decide to send in a review in which you describe your favourite restaurant and the reason it is special to you. You should also explain why you think it would be of interest to visitors to your area.
>
> Write your review in 280-320 words.

Target audience
You are writing this restaurant review for readers of a travel magazine who are interested in eating out. This is the general public and therefore it should be interesting, fun and not overly formal or academic. Typically reviews are written for a general audience.

Features of a review
Title
Every review needs a title. Plays on words are common in reviews, so a film review of *Harry Potter* could be entitled *Lights, Camera, Potter* or a film review *of American Pie 2* might be called *Another slice of pie*. It's

not always easy to think of something funny or eye-catching. Standby titles which always work, but might not be the most imaginative are:

- film: A night with (name of the star of the film)
- book: There is no friend as loyal as a book
- music: It's music to my ears
- restaurant: Come dine with me
- exhibition: A picture is a poem without words

Introduction

Reviews often begin with a short personal anecdote about why/where/with whom you did what you did. For example, *I don't often find the time to immerse myself in a good book, but on a rainy afternoon on holiday by the seaside I finally picked up 'The Life of Pi' by Yann Martel.* or *Weekend nights are made for eating out with friends. That is why last Saturday I found myself with two companions at 'The Vegan Table' in central Glasgow.*

Main body

The main body needs to be descriptive and include details about whatever it is you are reviewing. Most reviews have a clear narrative. If you are reviewing a book or a film, you should not include spoilers, for example telling your readers how the film will end. But you can talk about the ending in more allusive terms, for example *After a final spectacular plot twist there were audible gasps from the audience during the last scene. This thriller certainly kept the surprises coming right up until the end.*

Recommendation

In your recommendation you should clearly state why you are recommending this. In the case of a restaurant review or an exhibition you can also include the price, though you don't have to. For a restaurant it might be *Reasonably priced @ £25 per person for two courses with a drink.* For an exhibition it could be *Tickets start @£5 for students.*

Content points

You are given clear content points you must cover in this review. The content points for this question are

- you should briefly describe the restaurant

- you should explain why it is special to you
- you should explain why you are recommending it to others

The question also talks about a *local restaurant* so you should not review a chain restaurant.

Language

A review is the opposite of a report. You should give lots of detailed description, use colourful language and idioms if suitable, for example *the starters were to die for, the play featured a star-studded line up*, etc. You can write in the first person (*I, my, me*) though you don't necessarily have to. The language can be more informal and phrasal verbs are often used in reviews. Reviews are usually written in the present tense as you are usually reviewing something for others to experience (*The food is delicious* not ~~*The food was delicious*~~).

Now write your review. When you have finished writing your review, read through it and check your spelling and punctuation (capital letters, apostrophes, commas, etc.). Check subject–verb agreement, tenses and word order as well as singular and plural nouns. Make sure you have included all three content points and that your language is descriptive.

_____
_____
_____
_____
_____
_____
_____
_____
_____
_____
_____
_____

Ok, have you finished your review? Look at the sample answer and compare your writing. Would you want to eat in the restaurant you wrote about right now? If the answer is *Yes*, you've done a good job!

Sample answer: Part 2 a review

Here is the question again. Did you note down the same key words?

> A travel magazine is planning to run a feature on the best restaurants in your area and has asked readers for submissions on their favourite local place to eat. You decide to send in a review in which you describe your favourite restaurant and the reason it is special to you. You should also explain why you think it would be of interest to visitors to your area.
>
> Write your review in 280-320 words.

Now read the sample answer. Compare it to your answer. Are there any words or phrases you could use for your review? Try and add them to your writing to improve your answer.

Table for two

> Comment: A title referencing the name of the restaurant (The Gardener's Table)

The chilly winds, blowing ruby and amber leaves through our parks have left little doubt that autumn is finally here. Here in Stonebridge that can mean only one thing – it's time to head to *The Gardener's Table* to see what the inventive team in the kitchen have come up with using only the best produce from the autumn harvest.

> Comment: The opening paragraph sets the scene. The reader finds out the name of the restaurant, that the writer visited in autumn and that the cuisine is local and seasonal. Descriptive language to set the scene includes *chilly winds*, *ruby and amber leaves*, *only the best produce*, *the autumn harvest*. Useful phrasal verbs are *to head to* and *to come up with*.

And so my dining partner and I are heading on a blustery Friday evening to this cosy, family-run eatery on Main Street to sample their seasonal delights and warm ourselves by the roaring fire. *The Gardener's Table* has long held a reputation for being one of the most atmospheric restaurants in the region and it's easy to understand why, with its low beams, 16th century fireplace and rustic interior. I'm instantly reminded of the many enjoyable evenings I have spent here with family and friends. The dining room is at capacity but thankfully we've reserved a table. Given the season, we start our meal with pumpkin and garlic soup, a subtle, yet flavourful and soothing bowl of orange goodness. The knowledgeable server has recommended a light Sauvignon Blanc with this and we both agree that it complements the dish beautifully. For mains I opt for the mushroom risotto while my companion orders stuffed aubergine. Neither disappoints. The simple dishes are elevated by the freshness of the ingredients and the skill with which herbs and spices are used. Portions are generous, so instead of dessert we have two coffees to round the meal off.

> Comment: This paragraph covers several content points. The description of the restaurant includes both what it looks like, what they serve and the food. The writer also starts to mention why this place is special to them (they go there a lot with family and friends). The review is written in the present tense to make it sound more immediate (*my dining partner and I are heading …, I'm instantly reminded of…, we start our meal …*).Description of the restaurant is also in the present tense (*The dining room is …*). The present is contrasted with the present perfect for events that have happened prior but are still relevant (*we've reserved a table* [so we have a seat now], *the server has recommended a light Sauvignon Blanc* [which we are now drinking]) .The description of the setting includes *a blustery evening, the roaring fire, with its low beams, 16th century fireplace and rustic interior*. Useful language to talk about food includes *a subtle, yet flavourful and soothing bowl, a light Sauvignon Blanc, it complements the dish beautifully, dishes are elevated, the freshness of the ingredients, the skill with which herbs and spices are used, portions are generous, to round a meal off*.

Sipping on our coffees we see a sea of smiling, happy faces around us. *The Gardener's Table* is a local treasure, so many here are neighbours, colleagues and friends. However, a warm welcome is extended to everyone who comes through the heavy oak doors. Join us, experience the great produce Stonebridge has to offer. And if you're here in autumn, make sure to try the pumpkin soup.

> Comment: In this final paragraph the writer fully explains why this place is so special to them, but they also explain that everyone is welcome and that it's a great place to experience the area. This covers the final content point. There are some useful expressions with verbs in the text, such as *to extend a warm welcome, to experience something someone has to offer, make sure to try ...*

Part 2: set text essay

As discussed in the set texts section, you will be asked one question on each of the set texts. You may be asked to write an article, a letter, a report, a review or an essay. The guidelines already given on the article, letter, report and review apply to the set text questions. The set text essay, however, is slightly different to the essay in Part 1. Not so much in style, but in that you will not have two texts to summarise and evaluate.

Read the essay question on The Great Gatsby. Take a few minutes to think about how you would answer this question.

> **F. Scott Fitzgerald**
> *The Great Gatsby*
> 'Gatsby and Tom are pivotal characters in the novel. They differ in many ways, but are also alike.' Write an essay for your English language tutor. You should evaluate the extent to which you agree with this judgement, making reference to three or four particular events in the book or film.
>
> Write your essay in 280-320 words.

Have you noticed that the question asks you about the book or film? You can answer this question if you have seen the film and never read the book. However, you need to be very familiar with the film. Unless you have an excellent memory, it won't be enough if you've seen this film one time months ago. It should be clear from the question that you cannot answer it unless you are familiar with the book or the film. Do not try to answer it if you are not.

Structure

As in Part 1, your essay needs to be structured clearly.

Introduction
Your introduction should be short – about 20-40 words. It should state what the essay is about in your own words. Do not copy the words from the question. Paraphrase instead.

Main body
In the body of your essay you need to develop your argument. In this particular question you need to focus on the similarities and differences of two important characters from the book. The main focus should be

on how they are alike (The question states that *They differ in many ways* which suggests that the differences are obvious. But what are the similarities?) You should bring in your own opinions and clearly refer to several events in the book or film.

Conclusion
Your conclusion should be very short and simply sum up your main argument.

Language
As in Part 1, the language needs to be neutral or formal, but never informal. You haven't got the book with you, so you cannot quote directly, but you need to find ways of referring to the text. Do not say ~~On page 17 Gatsby states that~~… . Do say *Early in the storyline Gatsby states that* … . The passive voice is important in this type of essay. It's better to say *Tom is described as* … or *Gatsby is portrayed as* … than *Fitzgerald describes Tom as* … . As you are comparing characters your essay should be written in the present tense using high level adjectives (*reserved* not ~~shy~~, *crude* not ~~rude~~, *courteous* not ~~polite~~) to describe the characters.

Now write your essay. When you have finished writing your essay, read through it and check your spelling and punctuation (capital letters, apostrophes, commas, etc.). Check subject–verb agreement, tenses and word order as well as singular and plural nouns. Make sure you have included clear references to the book or film.

_____
_____
_____
_____
_____
_____
_____
_____

Have you focussed on the similarities and differences of the characters? Does your conclusion summarise your main argument? Would your English language tutor be able to follow your argument easily? If you've answered no to any of the questions, try to improve the essay before looking at the sample essay.

Sample answer: Part 2 set text essay

Here is the question again. Look at the underlined key words. Have you considered all these points in your answer?

> **F. Scott Fitzgerald**
> *The Great Gatsby*
> '<u>Gatsby and Tom are pivotal characters</u> in the novel. They <u>differ in many ways</u>, but are also <u>alike</u>.' Write <u>an essay</u> for your <u>English language tutor</u>. You should <u>evaluate the extent to which you agree with this judgement</u>, making reference <u>to the book or the film</u>.
>
> Write your <u>essay in 280-320 words</u>.

Now read the sample answer. Compare it to your answer. Did you have the same ideas or were yours different? How does your structure compare to the sample answer.

Gatsby and Tom are <u>key characters</u> in The Great Gatsby. <u>In most ways, the two men could not be more opposite</u>, but a deeper understanding of the book <u>reveals some similarities</u>, which are central to the plot.

> Comment: The introduction rewords the question (see underlined words) and gives the writer's personal idea (*which are central to the plot*).

Gatsby is portrayed as reserved, courteous and refined, despite coming from a humble background and working his way up. Tom's character is the polar opposite. He comes from 'old money' and has been wealthy all his life. Yet, he is crude, unpleasant and selfish. Physically Tom is a large, imposing man, whereas Gatsby is smaller and not always recognised at his own parties. He easily melts into the background, whereas Tom is overpowering with his booming voice. The differences are striking, yet there is one key figure tying the two characters together. They both love Daisy.

> Comment: This paragraph highlights some of the differences between the two characters. Notice the high level adjectives to describe the men (*reserved, courteous, refined, crude, unpleasant, imposing, overpowering*) and high level collocations (*humble background, polar opposite, old money, booming voice*).

Daisy is a central character to Gatsby and Tom. She's charming and beautiful, yet at the same time shallow and fickle. To Gatsby she is the single goal of all his dreams. He loves an idealised version of her and makes it his mission to win her back, as he has had a brief relationship with her in the past, before she married Tom. Tom loves her in his own way, though perhaps more as trophy. But perhaps even greater than their love for Daisy is their mutual fear of losing her. Even though Tom is at times unkind and cruel to Daisy, she is his wife. His pride would not survive if she left him. For that reason it is clear that the loss of Daisy could destroy him. However, she does not leave him and destroys Gatsby. Gatsby's death is ultimately caused by him trying to cover up Daisy's part in the accident. He is so afraid of losing her, that he takes the blame, which leads to his murder.

> Comment: The writer focusses on the similarities in this paragraph, which is the love for and fear of losing Daisy. Daisy's character is described followed by her significance to Gatsby and Tom and how this makes her the one thing they have in common. Detail about the plot is also given, making it clear that the writer has a clear understanding of the book. There are more high level adjectives (charming, shallow, fickle). Other useful phrases include *to make it my/your/his/her mission to ...* and *perhaps even greater than ... is ...*

Despite their many differences, Tom and Gatsby's commonality is Daisy. Their longing for her drives the whole plot forward, towards its tragic ending.

> Comment: The conclusion briefly summarises the key points of the essay.

Printed in Great Britain
by Amazon